THE GULF WAR
A Photographic History

Soldiers of the 1st Battalion the Staffordshire Regiment stand in a trench ready to attack during a live fire exercise in early January 1991. Notice the bayonets are fixed ready for close quarter combat.

The aftermath of war. An abandoned T54/T55 silhouetted against the flames from a burning Kuwait oilwell set on fire by Saddam Hussein's retreating forces.

THE GULF WAR

A Photographic History

MICHAEL DEWAR
and
The PRESS ASSOCIATION

ROBERT HALE · LONDON

First published in Great Britain 1992

ISBN 0 7090 4764 9

Robert Hale Limited
Clerkenwell House
Clerkenwell Green
London EC1R 0HT

Photoset in Century Schoolbook by
Derek Doyle & Associates, Mold, Clwyd.
Printed and bound in Great Britain by
Butler & Tanner Ltd., Frome, Somerset.

Contents

Operation Desert Sabre

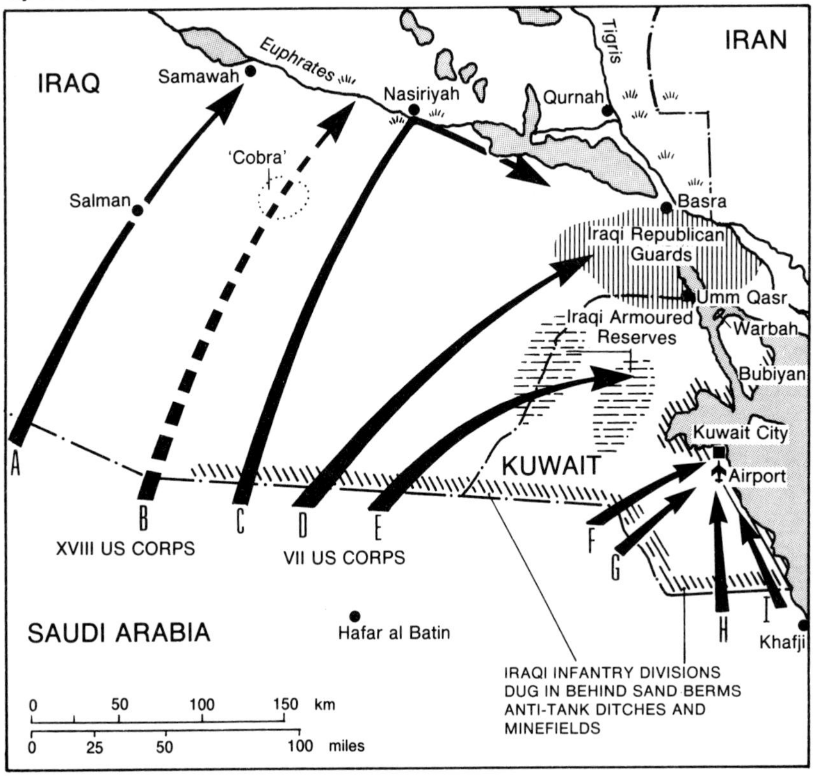

Key:

A – French Light 'Daguet' Division
B – 101st US Air Assault Division by Helicopter
C – 24th US Infantry Division (Mechanized)
D – 1st & 3rd US Armoured Division
1st US Infantry Division (Mech.)
E – British 1st Division
F – 1st US Marine Division
G – Combined Egyptian/Saudi Forces
H – 2nd US Marine Division
I – Saudi Forces

Map by courtesy of International Institute for Strategic Studies

Background to War

In the twelfth century the Muslim leader Saladin led the forces of Islam against the Christian Crusaders who had gained control of the Holy Land a hundred years before. Beginning in 1187, he won a series of decisive battles through a combination of daring, brilliant generalship, clever tactics and the incompetence of his opponents. Eight hundred years later the Iraqi leader Saddam Hussein, who saw himself as a latter-day Saladin, elected to lead Islam in a holy war which would once again free the Holy Land from the heretics. If he thought history was about to repeat itself he could not have been more wrong.

Saddam Hussein was born on 28 April 1937 in Tikrit, a small provincial town on the banks of the Tigris some one hundred miles north of Baghdad. His childhood was poverty-ridden and troubled.

President Saddam Hussein of Iraq was the central character in the entire Gulf crisis, he himself having initiated it in the first place. Unpredict able and frequently demonstrating signs of megalomania, he gambled that he would solve his country's many problems by invading Kuwait. In the event he merely increased them. Here Saddam Hussein answers journalists' questions during his press conference after meeting with Austrian President Waltheim who had come to negotiate the release of some Western hostages.

Finding anti-government activity more gratifying than studies, he joined the Ba'ath Party in Baghdad in early 1957 at the age of twenty. He was involved in an unsuccessful attempt on the life of Iraq's ruler,

General Abd Al-Karim Qassem in October 1959. He then spent a period in exile in Syria and Egypt returning to Iraq upon the overthrow of Qassem in 1963. The Ba'ath Party seized power in 1968, but it was not until 16 July 1979 that Saddam Hussein ousted President Bakr and assumed the reins of power and President of the Republic of Iraq.

In early 1990 Iraq's debts amounted to about £50 billion, most of this incurred by the need to finance the eight-year war with Iran. At the same time as having to manage this considerable economic burden – servicing this debt alone accounted for roughly 30 per cent of Iraq's projected annual income of £10 billion – Saddam Hussein was pressing ahead with a comprehensive reconstruction and rearmament programme. Inflation was increasing, a peace treaty had still not been signed with Iran, the Shatt-al-Arab waterway remained blocked and 70,000 Iraqi prisoners were still held in Iran. Clearly something had to be done to break this deadlock. Whilst the efficient apparatus of state repression could be relied upon to keep the people in thrall in the short term, another longer term solution to Iraq's problems would have to be found.

Pro-Iraqi Palestinian demonstrators hold aloft a picture of Saddam Hussein and burn tyres in protest against the Gulf War.

In February 1990 other events served to exacerbate Saddam Hussein's already precarious situation. A devastating indictment of his regime's human rights record was made public in the United States, presaging moves by the US Congress to impose economic sanctions on

Iraq. At the same time the main parties of the Iraqi opposition managed to show a degree of common purpose by meeting in London and declaring unequivocally that their aim was the overthrow of Saddam Hussein. All this coincided with the arrest, torturing and execution of the British reporter Farzad Bazoft for alleged spying in Iraq. This led to further widespread condemnation of the Iraqi regime in the West.

Then in March the 'supergun' affair, in which parts for what was apparently an ultra-long-range artillery piece were seized by the authorities in Britain and in transit elsewhere in Europe, alerted an increasingly concerned West to Iraq's weapons acquisition programme. If there was any doubt about such a programme it was quickly dispelled when a number of Iraqis were arrested in Britain for attempting to export what were alleged to be materials suitable for manufacturing a nuclear weapons triggering device.

Seen from Baghdad these events appeared to be a conspiracy hatched in the West and possibly even a cover for an Israeli attack on Iraq. In a defiant speech in April, Saddam Hussein characterized Iraq as the military champion of the Arab nation and, in alarmingly bellicose language, threatened retaliation with chemical weapons on Israel. At the same time he cleverly made the first of several conciliatory moves towards Iran signalling that he would be willing to settle unresolved issues outstanding from the eight-year war. Such an arrangement would of course allow Saddam Hussein to secure his eastern frontiers whilst he turned his attention to his Arab neighbours in the West.

His tactics became clearer at the Arab Summit held in Baghdad from 28 to 30 May at which he accepted Iraq's leadership of the Arab world and condemned the West – and the United States in particular – for propping up the Israeli state and undermining the Arab cause. His intention was principally to remind the Arab states of the debt they owed the Iraqi armed forces, both in the past against Iran and in the future against Israel. At that time at least half of Iraq's foreign debts were owed to other Arab states, in particular Saudi Arabia and Kuwait. It was Saddam Hussein's firm hope that the Arab States would come to his aid financially. Had they done so, much of the pressure would have been taken off the Iraqi government, the Iraqi people placated and Saddam Hussein's future survival assured. But he only succeeded in having the opposite effect, angering President Assad of Syria who did not even bother to attend the Summit, worrying President Mubarak of Egypt immensely and frightening the rulers of the vulnerable Gulf States. No aid or debt forgiveness was forthcoming.

What made matters even worse was that the May Summit marked the start of a period of steady decline in the price of oil, this having a dramatic effect on Iraq's actual and projected oil revenues. An inability

Some elements of the Kuwaiti ground forces managed to escape from Kuwait just ahead of the invading Iraqis. Here members of the Kuwaiti tank corps man their Chieftain tank somewhere in Saudi Arabia in November 1990.

of most OPEC countries to keep to production quotas was undoubtedly a contributory cause of this decline. However, Saddam Hussein chose to single out two particular culprits, Kuwait and the United Arab Emirates. A meeting at Jeddah on 12 July failed to impose the degree of discipline on these two offenders demanded by Iraq. A few days later Saddam Hussein accused both Kuwait and the UAE of flooding the oil market, of stabbing Iraq in the back and of helping the United States undermine Arab interests. It was then that he declared, 'if words fail to protect Iraq, something effective must be done to return things to their natural course and to return usurped rights to their owners'.

In that last week of July the seriousness of the situation was recognized, but the general interpretation of events, including that of the United States, appears to have been that Iraqi moves would stop short of military action. With the benefit of hindsight it is perhaps easier to see how events at this stage were moving inexorably towards war. Tariq Aziz, the Iraqi Minister of Foreign Affairs, had made some very specific demands in a memorandum to the Secretary-General of the Arab League. Kuwait was accused of setting up military positions in Iraqi territory and of stealing $2.4 billion worth of oil since 1980 from the Rumailah oilfield that straddled the Kuwaiti-Iraqi border. Kuwait was required to repay this sum and, together with the UAE, cancel all Iraqi war debts.

The Kuwaiti response was both defiant and uncompromising. It rebutted all Iraqi demands and accusations and, to rub salt into the wound, reminded the Iraqi government of the interest now due on its various loans. By 28 July there were 100,000 Iraqi troops massing south of Basra.

Incredibly US and other intelligence agencies calculated that Saddam was bluffing. This was also the perception at a hastily arranged meeting in Jeddah between Iraqi and Kuwaiti delegations to discuss all outstanding issues which ended on 1 August. In fact Saddam Hussein had probably decided in mid-July on invasion. He clearly calculated that the West, after an initial outburst of huffing and puffing, would not attempt to reverse a *fait accompli*. The dream of a greater Iraq beckoned. In the early hours of 2 August, Saddam Hussein's forces invaded Kuwait.

Operation Desert Shield

The Iraqi operation to capture Kuwait took approximately forty-eight hours. Armoured columns thrust south across the Mutla Ridge to Kuwait City which they had invested and captured within eighteen hours. Kuwaiti military resistance was brushed aside as Iraqi forces with an overwhelming superiority in both numbers and firepower secured all main centres of population and communications with virtually no opposition.

The UN Security Council was remarkably quick off the mark and, on the same day as the invasion, adopted Resolution 660 condemning the Iraqi invasion and demanding an immediate and unconditional withdrawal. The next day the Foreign Ministers of the Arab League voted by a majority to condemn the invasion, whilst the US concentrated on persuading governments to freeze Iraqi and Kuwaiti assets, halting oil imports from Iraq and Kuwait and convincing Saudi Arabia and Turkey to shut down the Iraqi oil pipelines that passed through their territory.

US Secretary of Defense Dick Cheney (*left*) and Chairman of the US Joint Chiefs of Staff, General Colin Powell (*right*) listen to reporters' questions at a press conference on 16 January 1991, the day before Operation Desert Storm began. Both Cheney and Powell were responsible for the planning and execution of the US and coalition war effort.

These efforts culminated in the passing of Resolution 661 on 6 August which imposed stringent trade sanctions on Iraq, excepting only medicine and, in humanitarian circumstances, foodstuffs.

The same day, the US Secretary of Defense, Dick Cheney, visited King Fahad in Riyadh with the purpose of offering US military support in order to protect Saudi Arabia's sovereignty and security. By this time Iraqi forces were massing on the Kuwaiti-Saudi border and it was beginning to look a distinct possibility that Saddam Hussein's next move would be a lightning dash southwards down the Gulf coast to seize oil installations and other strategic assets in Saudi Arabia. After some initial understandable hesitation about accepting the US offer, King Fahad readily agreed to the deployment of US troops on Saudi territory. On 8 August President Bush announced that US ground troops would be dispatched to Saudi Arabia on a mission which was, at that stage, entirely defensive.

In fact the earliest military moves had been made on a precautionary basis as early as 30 July when President Bush had ordered the aircraft carrier USS *Independence* with seventy combat aircraft on board to sail from the Indian Ocean, where it was on station, to the Gulf. On the same day he placed two squadrons of F-15 interceptors at Langley Air Force Base in Virginia on standby for departure to the Middle East. By 7 August they had arrived in Saudi Arabia and were being followed by further squadrons of F-16 fighter bombers, A-10 ground attack aircraft and five E-3 Sentry Airborne Warning and Control aircraft (AWACs).

It was to a large extent Prime Minister Margaret Thatcher's firm determination to resist Iraqi aggression that stiffened President Bush's resolve. Here she meets King Hussein of Jordan for talks on the Gulf crisis at 10 Downing Street on 31 August 1990. King Hussein was later to take an ambivalent stance during the war, walking a tightrope between a recognition of the justness of the coalition cause and his geographical position next to Iraq.

Operation Desert Shield was the code-name given to this deployment. During the following forty-eight hours they were joined by twelve Tornado F-3 interceptors, twelve Jaguar ground attack aircraft and a number of transport, in-flight refuelling and maritime reconnaissance aircraft from the Royal Air Force.

By coincidence the British Prime Minister, Margaret Thatcher, had been meeting with President Bush in the United States on 2 August. There is little doubt that it was her refusal to compromise in the face of flagrant aggression that dispelled any doubts President Bush may have had about the wisdom of standing up to Saddam Hussein. Thus it was that aircraft of the Royal Air Force were deployed in the Gulf only hours after US aircraft.

By 23 August approximately five hundred combat aircraft were deployed in the Gulf. They included F-111 long-range bombers as well as aircraft from the two US carriers now on station in the area, the USS *Independence* and the USS *Eisenhower*, with two other aircraft carriers *en route*, the USS *Saratoga* and the USS *Kennedy*. By the beginning of September the total number of aircraft had increased to 1,220. The first US ground units to arrive were elements of the 82nd Airborne Division and the 101st Air Assault Division, which closely followed the first aircraft arrivals on 7 and 8 August. By 15 August the first troops from Morocco and Syria had arrived, forces had been pledged by Egypt and Pakistan and the strength of US forces had risen to 25,000. These early arrivals were lightly equipped air mobile divisions which would have been at a disadvantage if they had been attacked by Iraqi armour before US armoured formations had deployed. Whilst the military build up continued, important political developments were taking place.

On 10 August a specially convened Arab summit in Cairo passed a resolution condemning the invasion, endorsing economic sanctions and pledging military aid to Saudi Arabia. Lined up against Iraq were the major Arab states of Egypt, Syria, Morocco and Saudi Arabia as well as all the smaller Arab states in the Gulf. Only Libya voted with Iraq against the resolution. Algeria, Yemen and the PLO abstained, whilst Jordan, Sudan and Mauritania entered 'reservations'.

Saddam Hussein had hoped to split the Arab world from the West but had failed dismally. Faced with the dilemma of how to escape from the consequences of his action, he decided to seize the initiative by unveiling his 'peace initiative' on 12 August. He stated that Iraq would agree to withdraw from Kuwait if Israel agreed to withdraw from the occupied territories and Syria agreed to withdraw from Lebanon. This was the first statement of the idea of 'linkage' which was to dominate much of the diplomatic manoeuvring which was to take place during the following months until the Iraqi government, faced with the prospect of total and devastating military defeat, suddenly abandoned its insistence on 'linkage' in February 1991. Saddam Hussein's intent was clearly to give the impression that the invasion of Kuwait was a means of achieving a much greater goal, the liberation of Palestine. This did have the effect of rallying public opinion across much of the Arab and Muslim world, but it failed to shake the resolve of the mainstream Arab governments which had stood out against Iraq.

More importantly none of the permanent members of the Security Council were willing to link the issues of Kuwait and Palestine in a form concrete enough to allow Saddam Hussein a way out of the dilemma he had created for himself.

Saddam Hussein's next move was to propose to Iranian President Rafsanjani in a letter on 14 August Iraq's terms for a settlement of the dispute between the two countries. These were in effect a return to the 1975 Treaty of Algiers which meant capitulation in the face of all Iranian demands. This climbdown by Saddam Hussein signalled a recognition of the gravity of Iraq's predicament. The intention appears to have been to clear the decks of all outstanding problems with Iran in order to allow all diplomatic efforts to be concentrated on the task in hand as well, of course, as freeing substantial numbers of troops stationed on the border with Iran for duty in the Kuwait theatre of operations. The price for Iraq was heavy: in particular it meant sharing the Shatt-al-Arab waterway with Iran since the Treaty of Algiers dictated that the international boundary should be the centre line of that waterway. Also the considerable numbers of Iranian prisoners of war would have to be returned as well as the sizeable tracts of territory seized from the Iranians in the border area.

Having, at a stroke, freed himself from the legacy of the eight-year war with Iran, Saddam Hussein decided the time was right to attempt to regain the initiative which was now so clearly with President Bush and the coalition which he was forming around the leadership of the United States backed by the authority of the UN. The Iraqi President ordered the detention of all the nationals of Western states in Iraq and Kuwait. The intention was to paralyse the will of Western governments should they be planning a military attack on Iraq, as well as force some kind of deal, or series of deals, with Iraq in return for the release of the hostages.

To some extent and at least for a time this seemed to work. A procession of Western politicians and public figures were seen to travel to Baghdad to plead for the hostages' release. Internally the resulting images on television were used to boost the image of Saddam Hussein who was seen to be playing a canny and apparently successful game with the West. In fact the effects of this strategy were almost entirely negative as Western public opinion became more and more outraged at

One of the losers in the Gulf crisis was Yassar Arafat, Chairman of the PLO who, by siding with Saddam Hussein, lost what little credibility he and his organization had remaining. Here he answers questions at a press conference in Amman on 16 February 1991.

It was President Bush's leadership and canny diplomacy which steered a shaky coalition through a seven-month crisis. He can hardly be faulted for the way in which he handled the series of challenges which confronted him during the crisis. His position as president is immensely strengthened as a result of America's success in the Gulf War.

continuing detention of innocent men, women and children. Saddam Hussein must have detected that the taking of hostages was not having the required effect. Thus he tried to have the best of all possible worlds by releasing certain categories: first certain nationalities, then individuals whose continued good health was in doubt and finally women and children.

It was not until December that he released all the remaining hostages at a stroke, presumably because he perceived that it was no longer to his advantage to continue to hold them. Anyway, by that stage there were other important considerations facing Iraq.

Meanwhile Operation Desert Shield was continuing apace. Following the passing of UN Security Council Resolution 661 on 6 August which called for the imposition of economic and trade sanctions against Iraq, a number of nations announced the dispatch of naval ships to the region. Eventually naval units were deployed by Argentina, Australia, Belgium, Canada, Denmark, France, Greece, Italy, the Netherlands, Norway, Spain, the United Kingdom and the United States, as well as non-combatant ships by Japan and Poland. A coalition naval presence was established in the Gulf, the Arabian Sea, the Red Sea and in the Gulf of Aqaba. A degree of co-ordination was achieved amongst European navies by the Western European Union (WEU) though the only two navies to take part in hostilities during the subsequent Operation Desert Storm were the US Navy and the Royal Navy.

Among the first to sail was a British minesweeping force, the first of a sizeable Royal Navy Task Force of some fifteen warships including, from January 1991, the aircraft carrier HMS *Ark Royal* which was deployed to the Mediterranean. By 15 January 1991, the US Navy had six aircraft carriers in the region, the battleships USS *Wisconsin* and USS *Missouri* and a large number of cruisers and destroyers. In addition, from early September 1990, except when it was engaged in assault landing training, the 4th Marine Expeditionary Brigade was kept afloat in the Arabian Sea. Moreover a second expeditionary brigade, the 5th, was available for amphibious operations from early January 1991. Even though in the event they were never used, their mere existence served to tie down large numbers of Iraqi troops to guard the Kuwaiti coast against the threat of a seaborne invasion.

On 25 August, UN Security Council Resolution 665 was passed which allowed member states to use limited force to enforce the economic sanctions which had been imposed by UN Security Council Resolution 661 on 6 August. The sanctions excepted medicine and, in humanitarian circumstances, foodstuffs. Resolution 665 also included the right to inspect cargoes. By this stage sufficient US and British warships were in place to enforce the blockade both in the Arabian Gulf

A Challenger tank of the Royal Scots Dragoon Guards, part of the 7th Armoured Brigade, boarding the Royal fleet auxiliary ship *Sir Bedivere* at Bremerhaven on 30 September 1990 *en route* to the Gulf. The logistic build up of allied forces was a feat of organization and planning.

SIR BEDIVERE
LONDON

Cook, Stephen Clark of HMS *Brocklesby*, saying goodbye to his wife Heather and four-month-old baby Roxanne when his ship, along with HMS *Bicester* and HMS *Brecon* left Rosyth Naval Base in Scotland bound for the Gulf. The British mine-sweeping effort was one of its most notable contributions to coalition naval forces.

and the Gulf of Aqaba. Ships suspected of carrying illegal cargoes to and from Iraq were systematically stopped and searched which meant that the blockade was almost immediately effective. This is not to say Iraq was immediately short of strategic materials, but certainly by December there were indications – with the imposition of petrol rationing – that certain vital goods such as petrol, steel and rubber were in short supply.

Eventually, perhaps, over a period of years, sanctions might have forced Saddam Hussein to his knees, but the ability of a primitive economy to survive in these circumstances is considerable. Whereas a doubling of the price of petrol could topple a government in the West, dramatic changes of circumstances can be circumvented in a command economy and by a totalitarian regime. Moreover, sanctions leaked over the Jordanian, Syrian and Iranian borders. There was never a shortage of foodstuffs. And also Kuwait was looted to such an extent that an additional supply of some goods resulted.

And finally there was so much redundancy in military equipment that it did not particularly matter if over a period of months there were no spares for 100 or 200 or even 1,000 tanks. With 5,500 tanks to play with, there was sufficient redundancy for Saddam Hussein to pose a credible military threat for years. Therefore, despite the best efforts of the coalition navies, economic sanctions were unlikely to work.

Time to Think. A nursing officer of 205 General Hospital waits for transport at her camp near Chester as over three hundred men and women of her unit prepare to set off for the Gulf the following day. They flew on 16 January 1991 just twenty-four hours before the onset of Operation Desert Storm bringing the number of British medical personnel in the theatre of operations up to nearly 6,000. In the event their services were hardly needed.

Injection practice for nurses Flight Lieutenant Julie Grunwell (*left*) of Harrogate and Flight Officer Debbie Calvert of Doncaster.

Nevertheless, they were rigorously applied. And, as the US and Royal Navies turned their attention more and more to preparing for hostilities, so the warships from the thirteen other navies which provided ships for blockade duties were used extensively for this purpose. The WEU provided a welcome degree of co-ordination for this task.

After the initial deployment of the 82nd Airborne Division and the 101st Air Assault Division in August, the US steadily built up their ground forces through September and October. Under the command of Headquarters 3rd Army was the XVIII corps consisting of the 82nd and 101st Division, the 24th Mechanized Division, the 1st Cavalry Division and the 3rd Armoured Cavalry Regiment, as well as the 1st Marine Expeditionary Force (less one brigade afloat at sea), the III Corps Artillery, the 11th Air Defence Artillery Brigade (with Patriot SAM), the 12th Combat Aviation Brigade and the 227th Aviation Regiment. This force was equipped with approximately 780 M-1 Abrams and M-60 tanks, 460 artillery pieces and 316 Apache and Cobra attack helicopters.

The British Prime Minister, Mrs Margaret Thatcher, announced on 14 September that the United Kingdom would send the 7th Armoured Brigade to Saudi Arabia. That this brigade was the successor to the 'Desert Rats' of the Second World War struck a certain chord in the United Kingdom. It arrived in theatre in mid-October and was initially

Challenger tank crews of the 7th Armoured Brigade unload their tanks from tank transporters in preparation for shipment to the Gulf in Bremerhaven on 29 September 1990. The Challenger tank distinguished itself in combat during the war.

Overleaf: HMS *Brave*'s captain Bob Williams (*left*), 43, and yeoman Archie Swales, 32, (*right*) watch anxiously as an Iraqi mine passes down the port side of the ship on 15 February 1991 at the height of naval operations during Operation Desert Storm.

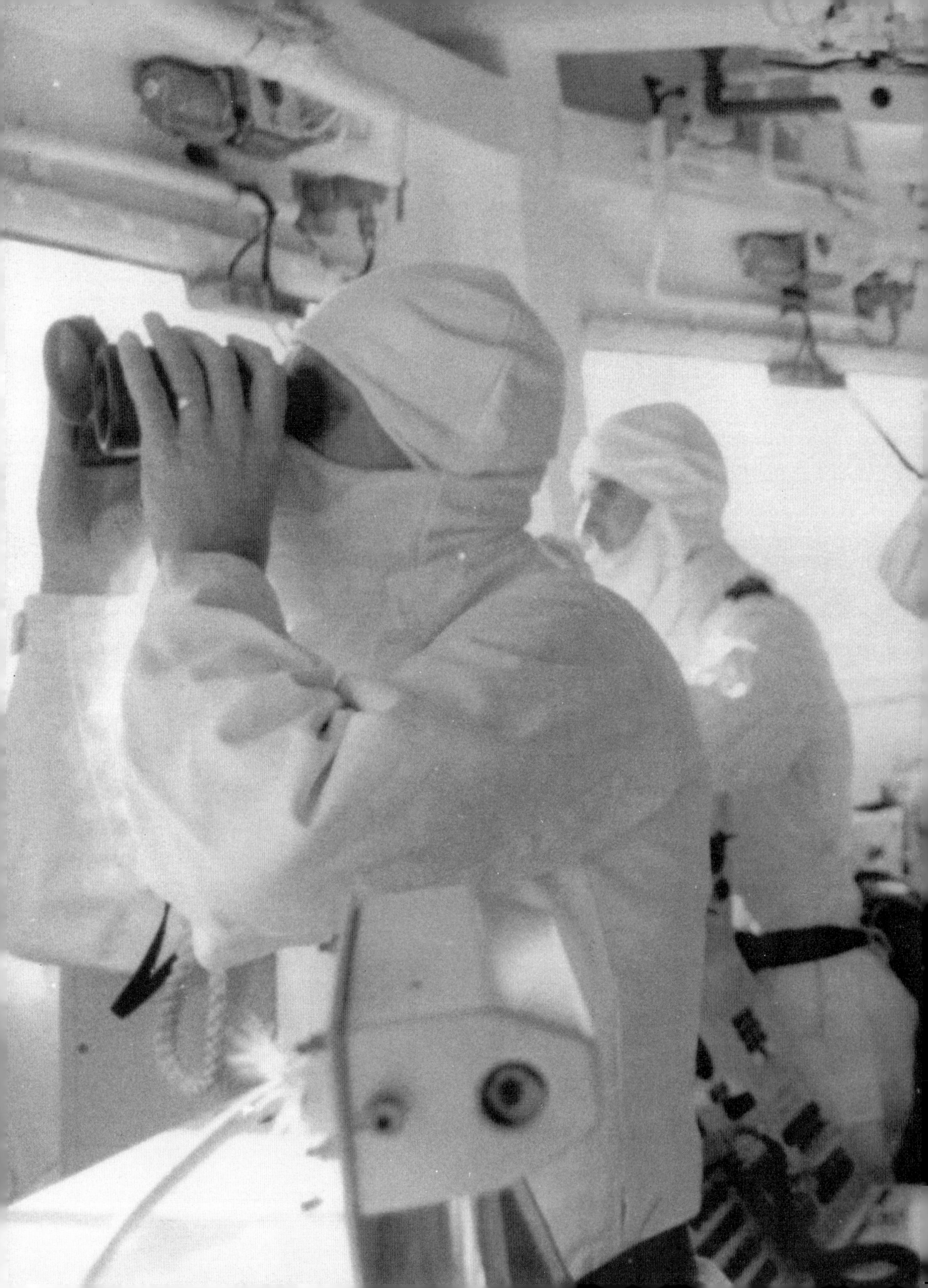

put under the operational control of the 1st Marine Division, though it was later to be put under the operational control of the VII US Corps. The British decision to send ground forces to Saudi Arabia no doubt played a part in the French also deciding to send a light brigade to join coalition forces, though the immediate cause was the temporary detention of the French military attaché in Kuwait and the occupation of the Ambassador's residence.

The watershed came on 8 November when President Bush announced that US forces would be more than doubled in the Middle East raising numbers of US troops there from about 200,000 to over 500,000. The XVIII Corps was joined by the VII Corps with the 1st and 3rd Armoured Divisions, the 2nd Armoured Cavalry Regiment and the 1st Infantry Division under command supported by other corps troops. The US Marine Corps strength was increased by the addition of the 2nd Marine Expeditionary Force ashore and the 5th Marine Expeditionary Brigade afloat. Main equipment strengths were thus increased at a stroke to 1,900 main battle tanks, 930 artillery pieces and 456 attack helicopters.

On 23 November, the British confirmed that they would more than double their strength by dispatching the 4th Armoured Brigade to form the 1st Armoured Division which would be supported by heavy

After Margaret Thatcher's downfall as Prime Minister of the United Kingdom in November 1990, Prime Minister John Major took over the responsibility for running the British war effort. This he did with great efficiency and some style. Here he meets US Secretary of State James Baker at RAF Alconbury during Baker's final tour of the coalition allies on 13 January 1991 just four days before the onset of Operation Desert Storm.

UK Defence Secretary Tom King (*left*) and then Lieutenant General Sir Peter de la Billiere (*right*), Commander of British Forces in the Gulf, answer questions at a press conference in London on 1 October 1990, shortly after the announcement that Britain would contribute substantial forces to the allied war effort in the Gulf.

artillery, armoured engineers, air defence and aviation regiments. The Division would have a total of 180 Challenger 1 tanks, 88 artillery pieces including 122 Multiple Launch Rocket System (MLRS) and 18 Lynx attack helicopters.

General Sir Peter de la Billiere was appointed Commander of British Forces in the Gulf. During his thirty-eight years with the Army, 57-year old Sir Peter served in Japan, Korea, Egypt, Jordan, Malaysia, Oman, Aden, and Borneo as well as in senior staff appointments in England. He spent thirteen of those years in the Gulf.

He joined the SAS in 1956 and later became Commanding Officer. He was then promoted to Commander SAS Group and finally became Director of the SAS. He masterminded the SAS raid on the Iranian Embassy in 1980. During the Falklands war he advised the Prime Minister on covert operations and controlled the SAS campaign.

He was mentioned in despatches after seeing action in Malaya, and then won his first Military Cross for leading SAS troops under fire in Oman. He was awarded the Bar to his MC for undercover SAS work in Aden in 1965 and after commanding operations in Oman from 1969 to 1974, he was awarded the Distinguished Service Order. His list of honours finally read KCB, CBE, DSO and MC.

The French force was also strengthened by the addition of an AMX-30 tank battalion and an artillery regiment and was designated the 6th Light or 'Daguet' division.

One of the two Lynx helicopters from RFA Fort Grange hovers in the background while Petty Officer Tony Gillie, 33, from the New Forest mans the general purpose machine gun on the flight deck of HMS *Brazen* on 28 February 1991. It was the Lynx helicopters armed with the Sea Skua missile which was so remarkably sucessful in sinking many Iraqi ships.

Members of a French helicopter combat unit masked against the effects of a sand storm on 3 February 1991. These French light troops proved particularly suitable for operations on the left flank of the allied offensive. They were highly mobile and ideally suited for the dash to the Euphrates.

Leading Airman Keith Ludlow manning the General Purpose Machine Gun on board a Sea King Mark IV helicopter from 846 Naval Air Squadron (normally based at RNAS Yeovilton) whilst on patrol over Gulf waters. Sea King helicopters would have been used to transport personnel from ship to ship and from ship to shore as well as landing parties of Royal Marine Commandos ashore for Special Operations.

The other main contributors to the coalition ground forces were Egypt and Syria, both of which provided substantial armoured forces. Much smaller contingents commited to the defence of Saudi Arabia were sent by Bangladesh, Czechoslovakia, Honduras, Hungary, Mexico, Niger, Pakistan, Poland, Senegal and Sierra Leone.

Air reinforcement of Saudi Arabia had of course been significant from the start of the crisis, simply because airpower is the simplest military asset to deploy quickly in a crisis management situation. But after the November decision to double coalition forces, the rise in the number of allied aircraft in theatre was dramatic. It needed to be, for the Iraqis enjoyed two important advantages in the air. They had a strong integrated surface-to-air defence system employing about 7,000 SAMs and 10,000 anti-aircraft artillery (AAA) pieces. They also operated substantial numbers of advanced combat aircraft totalling about 500. Of this number, approximately 50 were Soviet-built Mig-29 fighter-ground attack: 100 were French-supplied variants of the Mirage F-1; 25 were SU-24 and 60 were SU-25 ground attack. The remainder were older Soviet types such as the Mig-23/27 Flogger, Mig-21, Mig-25 and SU-20/22. Perhaps, most importantly, only a relatively small proportion

The coalition commander General Norman Schwarzkopf and the Saudi commander Prince Khaled bin Sultan talk to the press after ceasefire talks with Iraqi officers on 3 March 1991.

of these aircraft could fly and fight at night. But, on the other hand, the Iraqis possessed some 24 very large and heavily fortified main operating airfields and a further 30 major dispersal airfields. Most had runways 10,000 feet in length and covered huge areas. For instance, Talill air base in south-east Iraq was over twice the size of London Heathrow. The Iraqi air bases were also well provided with hardened aircraft shelters and all were protected with multiple SAMs and AAA.

Allied air power was therefore built up steadily during Operation Desert Shield so that by 18 January the allies had over 2,400 aircraft based either within the theatre of operations or close enough to be able to project power into it. These included not only the carrier-based air power from six US navy carrier battelgroups but also US aircraft (mostly F-111s) based in Turkey and US B-52 bombers based in Diego Garcia, Florio in Spain and Fairford in the United Kingdom.

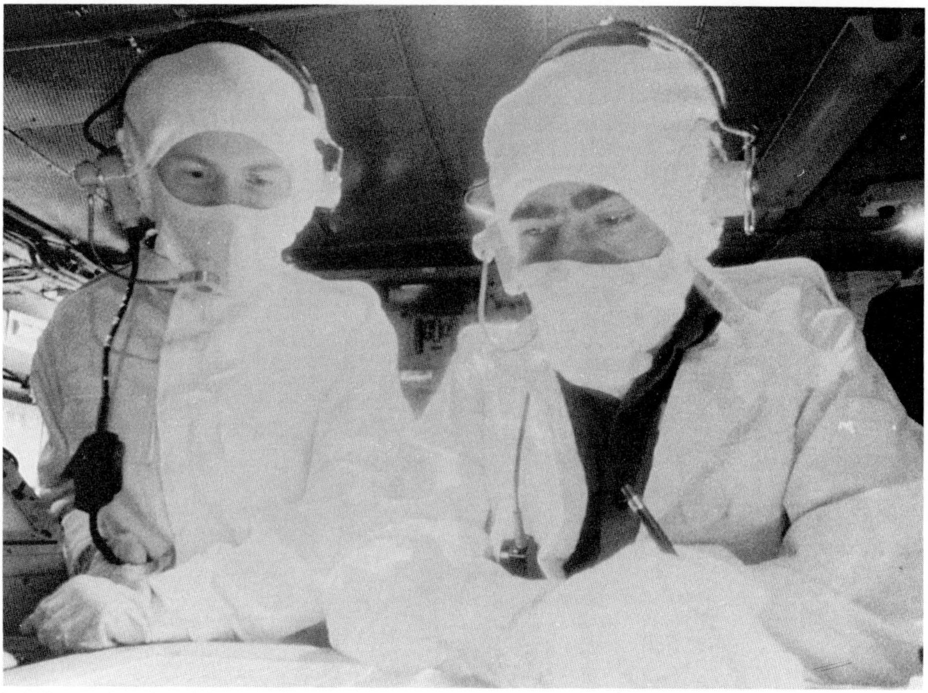

'Action Stations' in the operations room on board HMS *Brazen* in the Gulf on 16 February 1991.

Thus the build up of military power continued. The 8 November decision by President Bush to more than double allied power in Saudi Arabia thereby giving the allied commander, General Norman Schwarzkopf, an offensive military capability initially set off a storm of protest in the US. General Norman Schwarzkopf graduated from West Point, America's Sandhurst, in 1956, passing out 43rd from 485 officers, and took a degree in missile engineering. He served in Vietnam as a battalion commander where he was heavily decorated, including two Purple Hearts. It became clear he was being groomed for the top when he was appointed to com-

405
VFA-82

The bows of the aircraft carrier USS *America* loom above sand dunes as it passes along the Suez Canal *en route* to the Red Sea on 15 January 1991.

Overleaf: The Prince of Wales in a Challenger 1 tank photographed in December 1990 during a visit to troops in the Gulf.

91

mand the élite 24th Mechanized Division. He commanded the US Central Command (CENTCOM) when the Gulf crisis broke.

Many international critics insisted that the US President was forcing a war. The President countered that it was by no means certain that economic sanctions were bringing sufficient pressure quickly enough on Saddam Hussein to force him to withdraw from Kuwait and that economic sanctions must therefore be supplemented by the threat of the use of force. And the threat had to be a credible threat, hence the decision to double the number of troops.

However, much of the steam was taken out of any remaining criticism of the President by the passing of UN Resolution 678 on 29 November

US Secretary of State James Baker's shuttle diplomacy throughout the Gulf crisis demonstrated to the world America's resolve to avoid war if at all possible. Here he meets Saudi King Fahad bin Abdul Aziz on 5 November 1990 to negotiate the doubling of US troop strength in Saudi Arabia.

which authorized states to 'use all necessary means' against Iraq unless it withdrew on or before 15 January 1991. The vote was 12:2 with China abstaining and Cuba and the Yemen voting against. The passage of this UN Resolution largely satisfied allied public opinion that war, if it finally came, would be just.

To the last, Saddam Hussein sought a face-saving formula emphasizing again and again the linkage between the issues of Kuwait and Palestine. Whilst such a compromise seemed attractive to a minority, the coalition and the principal members of UN Security remained adamant that linkage was unacceptable, mainly because it would have been too great a reward for Saddam Hussein, particularly in the light of his brutal act of aggression, but also because it was impractical and would set a most unfortunate precedent for the future.

As the 15 January deadline approached, Saddam Hussein could not order an unconditional withdrawal for fear of appearing timorous and incapable before those he had put in positions of power in Iraq and upon whom he depended for his survival. Their support depended to a large extent on his capacity to deliver. And yet, as the last-minute meeting between US Secretary of State James Baker and Iraq's Foreign Minister Tariq Aziz in Geneva on 9 January made plain, Saddam Hussein was being required to make just such an unconditional withdrawal. The Iraqi leader had boxed himself into a hopeless position. There was no way forward or back.

The meeting between Aziz and Baker, at which Aziz contemptuously refused to accept a letter from President Bush to the Iraqi President, merely served to demonstrate the degree of Iraq intransigence in the face of world opinion. In the wake of this meeting President Bush requested the Senate to vote on an authorization for him to use offensive force if necessary. The vote was 52 Senators in favour, 47 against: not a wide margin but enough. Perhaps more important, public opinion was solidly behind the President with opinion polls consistently showing 85–90 per cent agreeing that the President should use force unless Saddam Hussein capitulated unconditionally by the UN deadline. The stage was set. The world held its breath.

Iraq launched SCUD attacks against Israel and Saudi Arabia in retaliation for allied air raids in an attempt to goad Israel into retaliating against Iraq and in order to break moderate Arab support for the coalition. Here a US soldier in gas mask and protective equipment and Saudi police officers examine the wreckage of a SCUD which landed in Riyadh on 22 January 1991.

Operation Desert Storm

At the end of the war, General Schwarzkopf gave a brief insight into coalition strategic planning considerations, when he said: 'Basically, what we started out against was a couple of hundred thousand Iraqis that were in the Kuwait theatre of operations ... [By November] huge numbers of [further] Iraqi forces had flown into the area. [By January] basically the problem was that they outnumbered us about three to two [and] in fighting troops ... two to one ... Any student of military strategy would tell you that to attack a position you should have a ratio of approximately three to one in favour of the attacker. And to attack a position that is heavily dug in and barricaded, you should have a ratio of five to one in favour of the attacker. We were outnumbered in tanks and artillery and we had to come up with some way to make up the difference. What we did of course was start an extensive air campaign' (*Strategic Survey, 1990-1991*).

Thus Operation Desert Storm was to start with a devastating air campaign. The aim was to remove Iraqi forces from Kuwait, therefore Iraqi ground forces had to be weakened and immobilized by direct air attack. Replenishment routes had to be cut. SCUD missiles had to be destroyed before their use could extend the war to Saudi territory and possibly Israeli territory. The resort by Iraq to weapons of mass destruction had to be prevented. Therefore targets within Iraq had to be attacked. Therefore air supremacy had to be established over Iraq and Kuwait as quickly as possible.

Overleaf: An Israeli woman is evacuated from the spot where an Iraqi missile exploded in Tel Aviv on 21 January 1991. Although they caused widespread panic, Iraqi SCUD missiles were extremely inaccurate and not in reality a particularly effective weapon of war. Although Iraq had the ability to arm SCUD missiles with chemical warheads she never employed this capability, presumably because she feared the likely political and military consequences.

On 23 January 1991, General Colin Powell, Chairman of the US Joint Chiefs of Staff, stated his plan succinctly: 'Our strategy for dealing with this army [in Kuwait] is very simple. First we're going to cut it off and then we're going to kill it. It is sitting there waiting to be attacked and attacked it will be'.

The 15 January deadline passed. The public US position was that the coalition was in no great hurry to implement the UN Resolution. In hindsight it is easy to see that this was part of an intentional deception campaign to reinforce Saddam Hussein's belief that the allies were

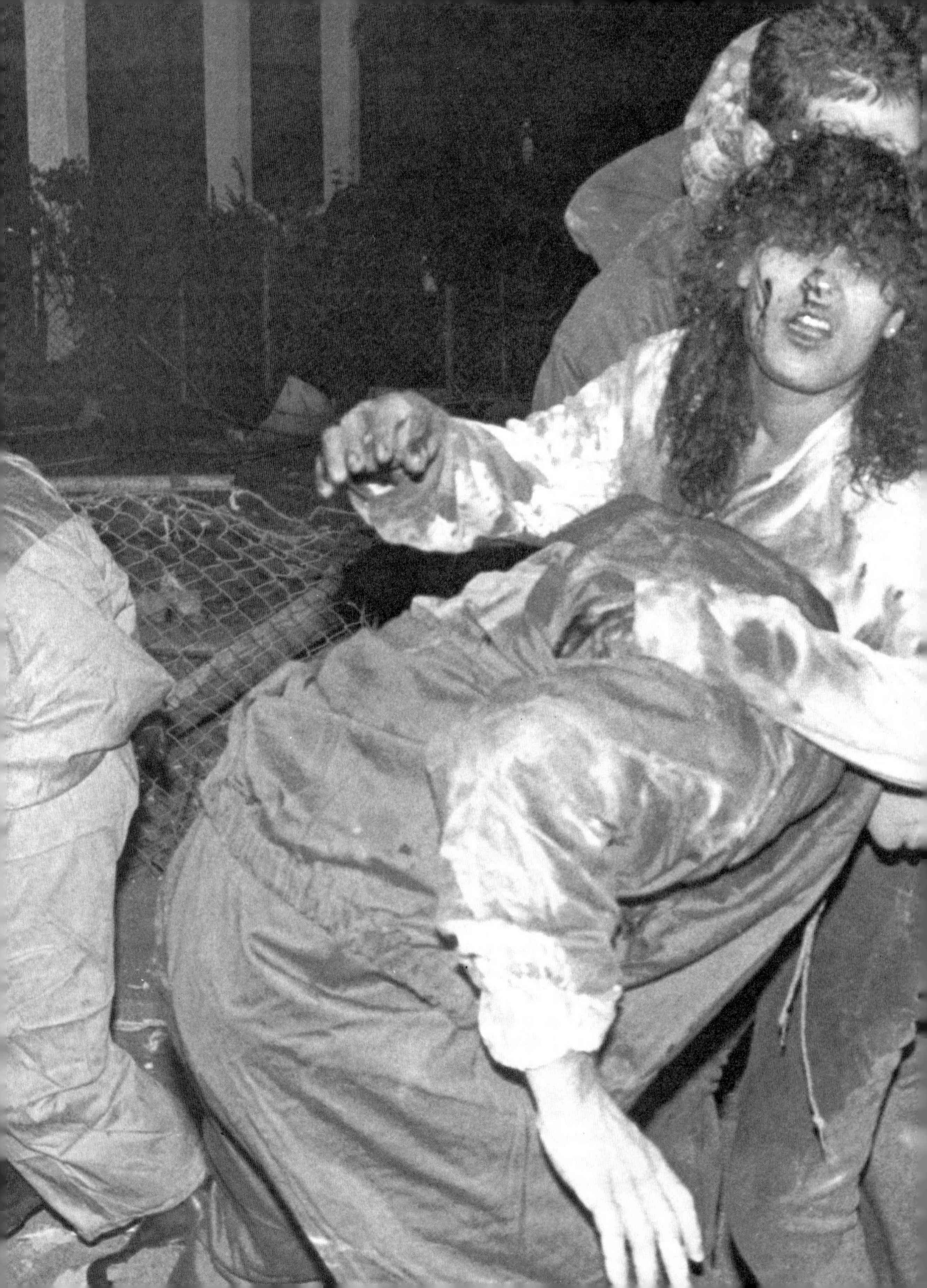

M1-A1 Abrams tanks of the United States 27th Infantry battalion forming part of the 24th Infantry division photographed during a pause in training in eastern Saudi Arabia on 28 October 1990. These tanks proved particularly effective during Operation Desert Storm.

STOP THE WAR! NOW!
CEASEFIRE NOW!
CHOOSE PEACE
STOP THE WAR
No blood for oil
COMMITTEE TO STOP WAR IN THE GULF
STOP THE WAR
CEASEFIRE NOW!
STOP
TTEE TO S

Support for the Government and its policy toward Iraq was remarkably consistent throughout the war. It remained in all public opinion polls at about 85 per cent of those polled supporting Government policy and the use of force, if all other means failed. There was, however, a small and vociferous minority who demonstrated in the streets of London throughout the war. Here, crowds march from the Embankment in Central London on 26 January 1991 in protest against the war in the Gulf.

unlikely to attack at all and, even if they did that it would be later rather than sooner and only then without risking heavy casualties, probably with an air campaign only. But General Norman Schwarzkopf had identified a relatively narrow window between mid-January when his offensive capability would be in place and mid-March when the Muslim holy season of Ramadan commenced. Even if that could to some extent be ignored, April saw the onset of unbearably hot weather.

In the early hours of 17 January the plan was implemented. Complete surprise was achieved by a co-ordinated attack employing Tomahawk cruise missiles and aircraft from the USAF, USN, RAF and Royal Saudi Air Force as well as Apache helicopters of the US Army. The Tomahawks, launched from US Navy ships in the Gulf, delivered 1000-lb warheads against Iraqi command posts, radar stations and chemical and nuclear installations.

The arrival of these missiles over Iraqi territory stimulated transmissions by Iraqi surveillance radars and surface to air (SAM) guidance radars, thereby disclosing their positions and making them immediately vulnerable to anti-radiation missiles and jamming. Thus the first manned aircraft to enter Iraqi airspace were EF-111A Ravens tasked to disrupt the Iraqi Air Force's response by jamming surveillance radars, the guidance systems of medium and high level SAMs and the airborne radars mounted in Iraqi interceptor aircraft. Surveillance and missile guidance radars were further confused by Tactical Air Launched Decoys. These are unmanned gliders, 10 feet in length with a speed of 300 m.p.h. and a range of 72 miles, which looked like manned aircraft on a radar screen and which could drop radar-calibrated metal strips – known as 'chaff' – to add to the overall jamming effect.

The final preparatory event took place in south-west Iraq when eight Apache helicopters attacked two Iraqi radar early warning and control sites. The Apache's target acquisition systems incorporating laser range finders, target designator and tracker, multi-power TV, magnified optics, forward looking infra-red scanner and night vision enhancement equipment enabled them to destroy precisely and surgically power generators, communications equipment and the radars themselves using Hellfire laser-guided missiles. Iraq was electronically naked.

At 0238 hours, 100 allied aircraft poured through the corridor that had been created *en route* to Baghdad and other targets. By 0300 hours F-117A Stealth aircraft were making precision attacks against high value targets in Baghdad. The ability of the F-117A to illuminate a target by laser allowed these aircraft to deliver bombs within one or two feet of the point of aim. Elsewhere USAF F-111s, F-15s and F-4s were attacking other command and control locations throughout Iraq supported by US Navy A-6s.

Meanwhile RAF Tornado GR-1 strike aircraft attacked airfield runways using the JP-233 runway denial system. Each Tornado carried two of these weapons which each contained 30 × 26 kg penetrating and cratering submunitions and 215 × 2.2 kg delayed action minelets designed to disrupt subsequent runway repair operations. The entire air onslaught was controlled by several E3A Sentry AWACs aircraft and air cover was provided by a round-the-clock presence of F-15, F-14 and Tornado F-3 air superiority aircraft which would have pounced on any Iraqi aircraft had they appeared. None did.

In the first 7 hours allied aircraft flew 750 sorties and as many again in the next 17 hours. The initial strikes were immensely successful giving the allies control of the air within 24 hours.

The first surface to surface missile (SSM) attack of the war was launched 24 hours after the allied air attack. Early on Friday 18 January, eight SCUD missiles were fired into Israel, six into the Tel Aviv area and two close to Haifa. Miraculously only a small number of people were injured. The next day both Israel and Saudi Arabia were attacked. The worst attack on Israel occurred on the evening of 22 January when 96 people were injured and three died of heart attacks. Throughout the war a total of 39 missiles were fired at Israel, mainly aimed at the Tel Aviv area. On two occasions missiles were fired at the Dimona Nuclear Weapons Research Station, but fell harmlessly into the Negev Desert.

More than 40 missiles were fired against Saudi Arabia from southern Iraq. Their targets were mainly Riyadh and the Dhahran area, but a small number were fired at Hafar al Batin, Bahrain and Qatar. The only really effective strike occurred on 25 February when, by an appalling stroke of ill fortune, a US Marine Corps barracks near Dhahran was hit killing 27 and wounding 90 Marines. SCUD missiles were extremely inaccurate and thus had limited military value, but as a terror and political weapon they were extremely effective.

The purpose of firing SCUDs at Israel was, of course, to draw Israel into the war thus making it extremely difficult for Arab members of the coalition to continue the struggle against Saddam Hussein. In the event Israel heeded US pleas not to react and showed remarkable constraint by remaining outside the conflict. In fact, even if she had retaliated, it is doubtful whether Egypt or Saudi Arabia would have withdrawn from the coalition. Indeed President Mubarek of Egypt indicated after the first missile attacks on Israel that Israel had the right to retaliate. But despite their military insignificance, the political impact of the SCUD missiles – with the attendant fear that chemical warheads might be used – was sufficient to warrant an enormous effort to both defend against them after launch but also more importantly to locate them on the

Iraqi civil defence workers and civilians inspect the damage near a Christian church caused by an allied bombing raid over Baghdad on 16 February 1991. Although some collateral damage was caused, it was quite remarkable how surgical allied strikes against targets in Iraq were. So called 'Smart' bombs riding a laser beam to their target allowed accuracies of between one and two feet.

A TV picture recording the moment when a laser-guided bomb dropped by a French Jaguar aircraft hits a concrete ammunition dump in occupied Kuwait on 2 February 1991. Providing the cross-hairs are kept on the target the bomb will follow the laser beam to the point of aim. *Right:* The target, a few seconds later.

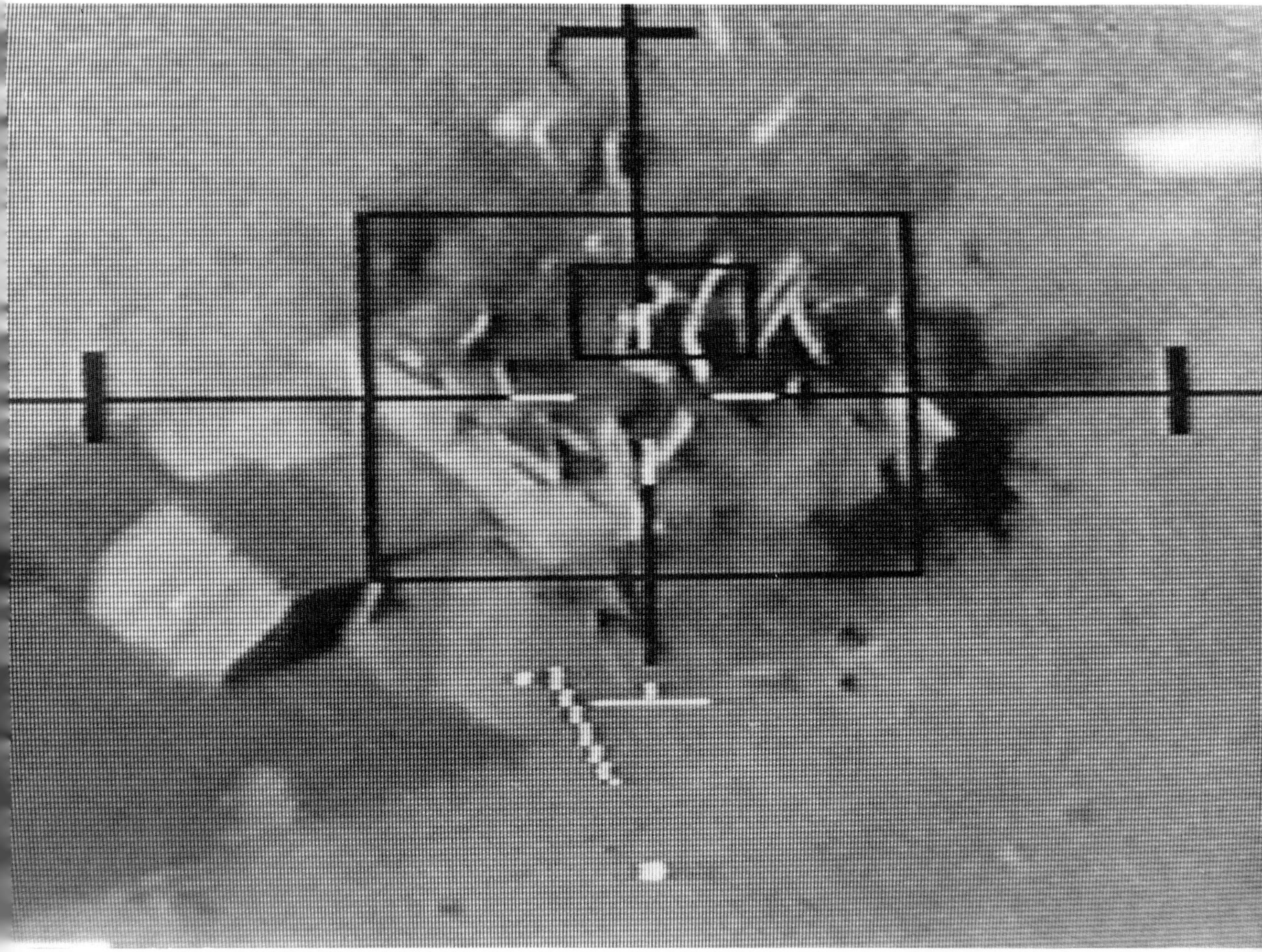

A 1,000-lb bomb is fitted under a Tornado bomber by Dave McLaughlin from Berwick-upon-Tweed, Scotland, on 21 January 1991, four days after the onset of the air offensive on Iraq. Tornados were employed dropping JP-233 runway denial weapons as well as 1,000-lb bombs on other targets.

American B-52 bombers played a leading role in bombing Iraqi armoured formations in the desert into submission. These aircraft were stationed on the island of Diego Garcia in the Indian Ocean as well as in Spain and at RAF Fairford in the United Kingdom. They flew non-stop missions from all three bases against the Iraqi Republican Guard entrenched in the desert. Their ability to drop massive tonnages of high explosives from a great height on an unsuspecting enemy was instrumental in breaking the morale of the Iraqi armed forces. Here a B-52 bomber arrives at RAF Fairford on 6 February 1991.

ground. The Patriot missile system was already deployed in Saudi Arabia but was also deployed very quickly in Israel. Although designed as an anti-aircraft system, its software had been upgraded and its fusing mechanism modified to give it some anti-missile capability. The system was surprisingly accurate with most missiles being intercepted though the debris resulting from interception often itself caused damage.

A comprehensive offensive effort was also mounted to tackle the SCUD threat at source. Mobile missile launchers are relatively large vehicles, somewhat resembling tanker trucks with a small train of supporting vehicles. They can nevertheless be relatively easily hidden in a suitable large building or even in deep road culverts. They normally moved to their firing positions after dark, fired their missiles and then returned to their hide before dawn. They were therefore extremely difficult to locate. The signature of their launch was seen by US surveillance satellites and this information transmitted to a satellite receiving station in north Australia with a direct link through to Riyadh. Nevertheless, by the time the firing location had been fixed there was sufficient time for the launched vehicle to redeploy to its hide position. But mobile SCUD

A Patriot surface-to-air missile in place in Saudi Arabia in October 1990. It was particularly effective in countering the SCUD threat. Although designed as an anti-aircraft missile, its software and fusing mechanisms were updated to provide an anti-missile capability.

launchers were successfully destroyed using 'SCUD hunting' combat air patrols and Special Forces.

The breakthrough came when Grumman E-8 Joint Surveillance and Target Attack Radar System aircraft (JSTARS) were employed. In late

Group Captain David Henderson (*left*) talks to Lt General Sir Peter de la Billiere, Commander-in-Chief of the UK Forces in the Gulf, during a visit to an airbase in February 1991 at the height of the air offensive. Note the fortifications of sandbags and oil drums filled with sand as protection against air or SCUD attack.

1990 two E-8s were still undergoing trials and had not originally been intended for deployment to the Gulf. However, General Schwarzkopf felt that the E-8 would be particularly effective in the desert environment of the Gulf and ordered their deployment in January 1991. The E-8 carried wide area surveillance moving target and synthetic aperture radars, producing images of ground force movements and fortifications at distances up to 100 miles at night and in all weathers. It relayed its information to the E-3 AWACs aircraft which instantly provided the necessary data for the 'SCUD-hunting' combat air patrols. These, usually consisting of four F-15 E aircraft, were allocated specific areas and gradually the SCUDs were destroyed.

By the end of the war eighty-one SCUDs had been fired and in the first month of Operation Desert Storm alone 1,500 sorties were mounted against them. It has also been confirmed since the end of the war that British SAS units and US Special Forces successfully engaged and destroyed mobile SCUD launchers behind enemy lines.

Overleaf: An RAF ground crew technician checking the inside of the enormous exhaust of a Tornado bomber at a Gulf air base on 9 February 1991. Maintenance crew worked around the clock to keep allied aircraft flying. Serviceability rates were remarkably high.

Whilst the campaign against the SCUDS was being waged, naval operations were also taking place. The first attacks on Iraqi naval units occurred on 23 January when a tanker, used as an offshore anti-aircraft position and a patrol boat were disabled, and three hovercraft sunk. Attacks on naval craft continued until 11 February when the last Iraqi

405
HMS
LONDON

patrol craft was destroyed. A large number of the Iraqi ships were sunk by Sea Skua missiles fired from Royal Naval Lynx helicopters. All the Kuwaiti patrol boats captured by the Iraqis were also destroyed. The Lynx/Sea Skua combination was particularly successful during this period, filling a capability gap that existed in the US Navy.

Naval gunfire support of operations ashore commenced on 4 February. This was undertaken by the battleships *Missouri* and *Wisconsin*, two recommissioned and updated Second World War US capital ships. Their fire was made devastatingly accurate by the use of Remotely Piloted Vehicles (RPVs) to direct naval gunfire support. These miniature aircraft flew over the target area transmitting live TV pictures of the target and allowing fire controllers to adjust fire accordingly.

The Iraqis made little attempt to attack coalition naval forces, though on 24 January a Saudi aircraft shot down two Exocet armed Mirages and on 25 February, Sea Dart missiles launched by HMS *Gloucester* intercepted a Silkworm anti-ship missile launched from the coast and almost certainly aimed at the battleship *Missouri*.

But the greatest naval contribution to the war effort was undoubtedly the provision of offensive airpower from the six US aircraft carriers as well as the devastatingly accurate Tomahawk cruise missiles fired from US battleships, cruisers and submarines. On 18 February two US warships were damaged by mines: the amphibious assault ship *Tripoli* continued on operations, but the cruiser *Princetown* had to be withdrawn to port for repairs. By 28 February some three hundred mines had been neutralized by allied minesweeping forces, a process which continued for several months after the cessation of hostilities.

The ground war was, to an extent, in the early stages a phoney war. The allies had selected the air option as their opening move. Therefore, with the exception of forward observation posts and patrols, the coalition ground forces were positioned well back from the Kuwaiti-Saudi border, out of range of Iraqi artillery. The front line – to the extent that it was a line – was held by Saudi Army and National Guard units and by other Arab forces from the UAE, Qatar, Egypt, Syria and Kuwait. United States, British and French forces were positioned some distance to the rear where they could both act as a reserve and carry out some very necessary desert familiarization training. The first US and British troops to arrive in the period before November were of course well-acclimatized and trained, but those arriving just before Christmas as a result of the November decision to double allied ground forces had had to work hard to achieve the highest levels of preparedness.

The first moves on the ground were made by the Iraqis who launched a number of probing attacks into Saudi Arabia on the nights of 29 and 30 January, four of which were not particularly effective. But the fifth, a

A Royal Navy Lynx helicopter with HMS *London* during a patrol in the Gulf of Oman on 12 January 1991. Lynx helicopters armed with Sea Skua missiles were responsible for sinking several Iraqi patrol boats during the conflict. It was an extremely successful weapons system filling a capability gap suffered by the US Navy.

A385

The Royal Fleet auxiliary tanker *Olna* (*centre*) refuels the newly arrived guided missile destroyer HMS *Gloucester* (*bottom*) and the supply ship RFA *Fort Grange* (*top*) in the Gulf of Oman on 28 September 1990. It was a Sea Dart from HMS *Gloucester* which later in the Gulf War intercepted an Iraqi Silk Worm missile heading for the US battleship *Missouri*.

A Sea Dart missile of the type launched by HMS *Gloucester* and which successfully shot down an Iraqi Silkworm missile aimed almost certainly at the US battleship *Missouri*. This was but one example of the close allied naval co-operation in Gulf waters throughout Operations Desert Shield and Desert Storm.

The guns of the USS *Missouri* fire at Iraqi positions ashore. Small remotely piloted vehicles were used to direct the fire of these guns accurately on Iraqi targets eighteen miles away. It was a measure of coalition naval superiority that these large ships could operate with impunity in the Gulf.

Airmen stand guard over RAF Tornado air defence fighters in Saudi Arabia in late August 1990. The Royal Air Force sent twelve aircraft from the 25th and 5th squadrons early on in the crisis to help defend Saudi airspace from Iraqi aggression.

US airforce ground crew load a Maverick missile on to an A-10 attack aircraft at a Saudi air base on 2 November 1990. Maverick missiles were highly effective tank killers and were tragically instrumental in the death of nine British infantrymen when a missile was accidentally launched at a British Warrior vehicle during Operation Desert Sabre.

Saudi Tornados at Dahran air base on 22 August 1990. US and British aircraft operated from Dahran air base alongside their Saudi counterparts.

BA

Previous page: RAF Tornado GR1 bombers lined up on an airfield in Bahrain; it was these aircraft which were later to mount bombing missions against Iraqi airfields and other targets.

Two Tornado jets refuelling from a Victor tanker on their way to Dahran on 17 September 1990. The jets needed to repeat the 450 m.p.h. manoeuvre four times in order to complete the 4,000-mile trip non-stop. It was this mid-air refuelling capability which gave coalition aircraft one of several advantages throughout the Gulf War.

brigade-sized force, achieved a degree of surprise and caught the allies off balance. In the early hours of the 30th the Iraqi armoured column thrust southwards from its position in Kuwait and occupied the small Saudi town of Khafje situated just eight miles from the border.

The town had been evacuated some two weeks previously when it came under Iraqi artillery fire. Part of the oil storage facility in the town had been set on fire and a pall of black smoke had hung over the town for days. All the world knew that Khafje was empty and unoccupied: images from the deserted town had appeared on TV in Europe, in the United States and most certainly in Iraq. US Marine patrols perhaps ten men strong were seen motoring around the town during daylight hours. But it was quite apparent that the town was deserted and, more important, undefended.

The Iraqis, who by this stage had suffered nearly two weeks of unremitting attack from the air and whose air force had been effectively neutralized, had no sophisticated means of gathering intelligence. The allies knew what was happening twenty-four hours a day throughout the Kuwaiti theatre of operations having at their disposal satellite imagery, photo reconnaissance aircraft, Remotely Piloted Vehicles, E3 Sentry AWACs aircraft, Sideways Looking Radar, the new JSTARS system, special forces patrols behind enemy lines and other systems besides and were awash with information about the enemy. The Iraqis, on the other hand, were electronically blind and deaf. Thus when presented with the clear statement on TV that Khafje was undefended and, needing some sort of success to bolster flagging morale, the Iraqis struck.

So as to remain out of artillery range the northernmost allied positions were well south of the town. A vacuum existed and Saddam Hussein's forces were quick to fill it. They moved too quickly for the allies to make a meaningful counter move. There was much press criticism at the time of the fact that the allies had been taken by surprise. But it was ill informed. It failed to appreciate that an armoured column could suddenly emerge from behind enemy lines where it had been lost on a radar screen in the 'noise' of all the other enemy formations, and move the fifteen kilometres to Khafje far too quickly to be stopped if there were no troops actually occupying the ground through which they were moving. Nevertheless it was a suicidal mission from the outset, but the press, of course, saw it as a great public relations coup for Saddam Hussein. And, indeed, in a way it was. The allies were caught off balance; they were not expecting such a move and it caused some embarrassment.

Once the Iraqi forces consisting of approximately 2,000 men and 50 tanks had consolidated in the small border town, they became extremely difficult to dislodge. Any approach across the featureless terrain towards the town was spotted by the Iraqis holding the perimeter of the built up area. Thus, the Saudi and Qatari troops in the surrounding desert found that they came under intense fire every time they attempted to approach the town.

General Schwarzkopf in the Coalition Headquarters in Riyadh took two decisions very quickly: first, the town would be retaken by the Saudi Army with the support of Qatari troops in the area. It was Saudi soil, therefore Saudis must be seen to defend their own territory. This would send an important political message to the Arab world in particular. Second, there would be no unnecessary loss of life amongst coalition forces in the retaking of the town. Militarily the Iraqi offensive was of no significance whatsoever. Therefore they would be removed methodically and when the moment was right.

The Iraqi force in Khafje was equipped with T54/T55 tanks and BMP armoured personnel carriers. They were in range of their supporting artillery to the north of the Kuwaiti border and, since Khajfe was on the coastline, they could be supported or reinforced by Iraqi naval forces. If the Iraqi air force chose to fly they were well within range of Iraqi close support aircraft. There was the potential therefore for causing considerable and prolonged embarrassment to the coalition. But the Iraqi attack was ill co-ordinated and not really pressed home with sufficient support. A force of Iraqi patrol craft and landing craft was intercepted by US and British naval forces heading south along the coast towards Khafje on 30 January. These were engaged by ship-launched helicopters and aircraft and were all destroyed or beached following the coalition attack. It is probable that this force was attempting to reinforce or resupply the Khafje land forces.

By the time coalition forces had recovered from the initial shock of the attack, they were able to start planning counteraction. The priority was to ensure that the Iraqi bridgehead was not consolidated. British, and US aircraft were scrambled to interdict the Iraqi lines of communication between Khafje and the Kuwait border, thus ensuring that no further Iraqi armoured columns entered the battle. British Jaguar ground attack and US A-10 Thunderbolt tank killers in particular took on Iraqi forces north of Khafje. Meanwhile, US Marine Corps 155-mm artillery and Cobra attack helicopters completed the ring of steel that was thrown around the small town. The artillery engaged reinforcements attempting to move south and stragglers attempting to move north from the town. The Cobras fired their TOW anti-tank missiles at armoured targets that appeared fleetingly in the town.

But the only way in which the Iraqi force could be defeated was to move into the town, engage them in close quarter combat and defeat

British soldiers of the Royal Scots forming part of the 4th Armoured Brigade stand in front of their Warrior mechanized combat vehicle somewhere in Saudi Arabia on 7 January 1991. These infantrymen are equipped for battle. The soldier on the right is carrying the SA80 assault rifle and the soldier second from the right the light support weapon (LSW).

A pair of Jaguars lift off from a Gulf air base to attack the occupied Saudi border town of Khafje early on 31 January 1991. It was largely US and British air support which enabled Saudi and Qatari troops to recapture Khafje relatively quickly.

French officers inspect a destroyed Iraqi T54/T55 tank on 25 February 1991. The bulk of the Iraqi tank force comprised this type of tank, an old but reliable Soviet-built tank but one which was no match for the much more modern tanks of the coalition forces.

A member of the RAF regiment guarding a Rapier surface-to-air missile site at an airfield in the Gulf on 20 January 1991. These missiles were never used in anger during the war since no Iraqi aircraft attacked coalition airfields.

them. It took the Saudi and Qatari troops some hours to move into position but they were able to launch a counter attack late on the 30th by which time the Iraqis had been in possession of the town for nearly twenty-four hours. Saudi and Qatari troops used the cover of darkness to gain a lodgement on the southern edge of the town after nightfall on the 30th. Since the layout of Khafje is open and the town consists of low modern buildings, the problems associated with gaining entry to a dense environment did not exist. Moreover, the civilian population had been evacuated and thus there was no danger of causing innocent loss of life. As the leading AMX-30 Qatari and M-60 Saudi tanks moved forward supported by infantry in armoured personnel carriers as well as by artillery fire and attack helicopters, they met small arms and anti-tank fire but it was inaccurate and sporadic. A lodgement was achieved relatively quickly but the Iraqis then proceeded to provide relatively stiff opposition. Groups of Iraqi infantrymen had to be winkled out of the mostly single-storey buildings. Whilst some caused serious delay to the progress of the coalition forces, many more surrendered. But there were pockets of furious resistance. The Saudis lost several armoured personnel carriers, 32 wounded and 15 dead. But casualties were much more serious for the Iraqis. They lost 42 tanks, all T54s, and 40 dead, many of these in the destroyed tanks. 500 Iraqi prisoners of war were taken. The remainder of the invading Iraqi force managed to make it back, one way or another, along the coastline northwards to Kuwait. The corridor they had created was never entirely closed. Although a brigade had launched the original attack, only some 600 Iraqis attempted to hold the town until the end.

The town was declared clear on 1 February, though it took until the 3rd to eliminate the odd lone sniper who refused to surrender.

On 12 February the coalition forces began an artillery bombardment of Iraqi defensive positions along the whole length of the front. Although this was initially sporadic it increased in intensity as February progressed. The US and British armoured divisions were equipped, in addition to their conventional artillery, with the devastating Multi Launch Rocket System (MLRS). Apache helicopters joined A-10 tank killers to further reduce Iraqi tank and artillery strength. It was also at this stage that B-52 raids against Iraqi troop concentrations were increased in intensity. And all the while Allied Ground forces secretly manoeuvred in preparation for the ground assault.

Operation Desert Sabre

At 0400 hours (Kuwait time) on Sunday 24 February Operation Desert Sabre began. In accordance with an elaborate deception plan, the first attacks were by two US marine divisions and Saudi, Egyptian and other Arab forces north across the border into Kuwait. In conjunction with more marines afloat in the Gulf which appeared to be threatening the Kuwaiti coastline, the deception plan was designed to give the impression that the coalition attack was a simple thrust directly into Kuwait.

The crew of a Scimitar reconnaissance vehicle watch the progress of other vehicles during a live firing exercise in January 1991. During the waiting period before the ground assault coalition forces trained extensively, honing their professional skills to the highest possible standard.

In the weeks before the ground offensive the allies had manufactured a grand charade using airpower, offensive patrolling, artillery bombardment, troop deployments and bogus radio traffic to suggest that the main allied thrust was going to be across the Saudi/Kuwait border supported by an amphibious landing in the Northern Gulf. All the while an envelopment on a grand scale a hundred miles to the west

A lone US soldier guards recently captured Iraqi soldiers on 25 February 1991. They are awaiting transport to take them to a POW camp. Whilst most Iraqi prisoners were in reasonable physical shape upon capture, there is little doubt that their morale after weeks of shelling and bombing was at a very low point.

A batch of Iraqi prisoners of war is shepherded by Saudi Arabian soldiers towards captivity.

Engineers of the 82nd Airborne division demolish an Iraqi bunker next door to a T54 Iraqi tank on 25 February 1991 deep inside Iraq.

Overleaf: A US marine searches an Iraqi prisoner on 26 February 1991, during the advance on Kuwait City.

The scene in January 1991 during a live firing exercise in the Saudi Arabian desert during which tanks practise engaging targets at night using the light of flares.

TOYOTA

was being planned. And when it took place it achieved total surprise. It demonstrated a degree of speed, mobility and sheer military brilliance that proved to be beyond the comprehension of the Iraqi military mind. It was pure blitzkrieg.

Massive armoured forces cut through southern Iraq to within 150 miles of Baghdad in hours. With their air force neutralized and their command, control and communications (C^3) system crippled, the Iraqis were electronically blind and deaf. The British 1st Armoured Division played a crucial part in this outflanking or envelopment movement. Its precise role was to strike north across the Saudi/Iraq border with US and French forces to its west. Then it was to turn eastwards and hit Iraqi reserve formations in the flank which were situated in the area of the north-west corner of Kuwait.

Throughout 25 and 26 February, the US VII Corps closed with and attacked Iraqi Revolutionary Guard positions along the western Kuwait border. The 1st British Armoured Division were in the vanguard of this action. On 27 February, coalition forces entered Kuwait City in triumph.

Meanwhile, the 1st Armoured Division continued to engage retreating Republican Guard divisions in the desert. At 1700 hours that day General Schwarzkopf in his daily briefing announced that 29 Iraqi divisions were combat ineffective, that 3,700 Iraqi tanks had been destroyed and that US ground casualties were 29 killed in action, 213 wounded and 44 missing.

Tragically that day the British 1st Armoured Division suffered mistakenly its first fatalities in action when a US A-10 Thunderbolt aircraft attacked a Warrior armoured vehicle killing 9 members of the Staffordshire Regiment. It was, of course, a tragedy but in the fog of war and heat of battle this sort of accident is all too commonplace. In the Falklands conflict a British warship had shot down an Army helicopter, the Scots Guards had fired on RAF fighters and British ground forces had opened fire on their own patrols.

'The Mother of all Battles' – a phrase originated by Saddam Hussein – as US Defense Secretary Cheney put it, was turning into 'the Mother of all Retreats'. Throughout 27 February, British ground forces were engaged in heavy fighting as the Challenger Regiments chased the retreating Iraqis in a north-easterly direction towards the Iraqi city of Basra. The Challenger 120 mm guns proved highly effective and extremely accurate firing at ranges in excess of 2,000 metres and scoring hit after hit. The Soviet-built T-72 tanks manned by the Republican Guards proved no match for the lethal APFSDS (Armour Piercing Fin Stabilized Discarding Sabot) rounds fired by Challenger. Iraqi tank hulks littered the desert, a macabre testimony to the military ambitions of Saddam Hussein. The British tanks were supported by US A-10 'tank-busting' aircraft as well as RAF Jaguar ground attack jets. The Multi Launch Rocket System (MLRS) manned by the Royal Artillery was devastatingly effective. Before tank and infantry units engaged the enemy in close combat, the way was prepared by salvoes from the MLRS launchers. Every tracked MLRS launcher had two pods, each with six rockets. Each rocket contained 644 bomblets filled with high explosive. The range of the system was 32,000 metres and one launcher is capable of firing twelve rockets inside a minute. The weight of fire that can be delivered on the ground proved to be totally overwhelming, to the extent that Iraqi artillery stopped returning fire. They appreciated that, if they did, artillery locating radar would pinpoint their position and that within minutes an MLRS salvo would land on their positions.

Iraqi Foreign Minister Tariq Aziz arrives in Moscow for talks with President Mikhail Gorbachev and Foreign Secretary Bessmertnykh (*left*) on 18 February 1991. Tariq Aziz faithfully followed his president's policies to the last. The Soviets, keen to find a peaceful solution to the crisis, tried to the very end to persuade the Iraqis to see sense.

Whilst the battle raged, Saddam Hussein desperately tried to extricate himself from his predicament. Even to him, by 26 February the outcome was not in doubt. Characteristically, he tried to salvage something through diplomacy. He announced that Iraqi forces were 'withdrawing' from Kuwait. He called on the Security Council to allow a 'dignified withdrawal'. His request was rejected by the Security Council which insisted that Saddam Hussein accept all the UN Resolutions.

On 27 February Tariq Aziz tried again announcing that Iraq was withdrawing 'in accordance with UN Resolutions' and requesting that sanctions be lifted. Aziz was told that only one sentence was required

Overleaf: A scene of utter devastation on the Mutla Pass north of Kuwait City where hundreds of Iraqi tanks and vehicles were caught by allied aircraft fleeing to Iraq. This photograph was taken after the end of hostilities.

accepting all UN Resolutions unconditionally.

That same day, Iraqi forces were caught on the Mutla Pass north of Kuwait City in headlong retreat towards Basra by allied airforces. It was total slaughter with aircraft making pass after pass and destroying hundreds of vehicles. The graveyard of men, vehicles and equipment that resulted is one of the enduring and most horrific images of the war. On 28 February, Tariq Aziz said that Iraq was ready to 'comply fully with Resolution 660 and all UN Resolutions on Kuwait'. President Bush immediately ordered a ceasefire to take place at 0800 hours Kuwait time exactly one hundred hours from the launch of the ground offensive. Operation Desert Sabre had run its brief course.

At this stage over 4,000 Iraqi tanks had been destroyed, 42 divisions captured, destroyed or rendered combat ineffective and 80,000 prisoners of war taken. Some 15–20,000 Iraqi troops remained in fighting formations in the Kuwaiti theatre of operations when the ceasefire was declared. The exact number of Iraqis killed in action will almost certainly never be known. Saudi military sources estimated that 100,000 were killed, others said 25–50,000. It is likely that the figure was higher rather than lower.

The victory achieved by the coalition ground forces in one hundred hours of combat, and by the 1st British Armoured Division in particular, was undoubtedly one of the greatest military achievements of all time. Why was it so complete and why did so many experts predict that it would be much more difficult to achieve? Neither politicians nor

Coalition commander General Norman Schwarzkopf salutes Iraqi Lieutenant General Sultan Hasheem Ahmad after the ceasefire talks at an Iraqi base in southern Iraq on 3 March 1991.

Overleaf: The stark reality of war. The charred bodies of Iraqi soldiers lie in grotesque disorder following a cluster bomb attack on their convoy near the Iraq-Kuwait border in February 1991.

military commanders would have been forgiven if the Iraqi war machine had been *underestimated*, so instead it was taken at face value and worst case scenarios were generated.

It is easy with hindsight to state that it was always obvious that the Iraqi army was no match for the coalition. The fact was that it was the fourth largest army in the world. It included 5,500 tanks, over a million men, 3,500 artillery pieces and was supported by an air force of over 750 combat aircraft. Moreover, its inventory included ballistic missiles and a comprehensive chemical arsenal which it had used during the Iran-Iraq war and against innocent Kurdish villagers in 1988. It was for this reason that the coalition built up its strength to in the region of 737,000 men, 190 ships and 1,700 combat aircraft.

In the event, victory was achieved with relative ease. This was for a number of reasons. First, allied air supremacy had exacted an enormous toll on the Iraqis during the six weeks of the air offensive. Second, coalition intelligence arising from this air supremacy was a crucial asset. Third, the technological edge held by the allies in terms of equipment, command and control facilities and logistic support meant that the Iraqis were fighting in a different league with systems that were for the most part a generation out of date. Fourth, the level of training and expertise amongst the professional armies of the coalition allowed them to outthink, outmanoeuvre and outfight the Iraqi Army and last, and most important, the whole style of warfare fought by a western military machine – as compared to the Soviet style adopted by the Iraqis – gave the coalition a massive advantage. The Iraqis favoured static warfare behind fixed defences controlled by a rigid, hierarchical command structure whereas the western (essentially NATO) system was based on the Air Land Battle concept of manoeuvre warfare. Instead of rigid orders obeyed to the letter, Air Land Battle envisages the issue of broad directives which can be interpreted as more junior commanders see fit for that particular moment of the battle. Thus subordinate commanders are permitted to show initiative and react to a particular situation, *providing* they remain within the broad parameters set by the overall commander.

The Royal Saudi Air Force is a modern, well equipped force consisting of some 250 combat aircraft, mostly US-manufactured F-15C and F-5E fighters and British-manufactured Tornado fighter-bombers. Here mechanics ready an F-15 for a mission at an airbase in Eastern Saudi Arabia in late January 1990.

General Peter de la Billiere. He was called back from retirement by Prime Minister Margaret Thatcher two days before he was due to leave the service. His distinguished record in the Special Forces and in other capacities in the British Army over many years all over the world made him an ideal candidate for this appointment.

A US marine (*centre*) celebrates with Kuwaiti citizens on the top of the police station in Sabahiah on 26 February 1991 during the advance on Kuwait City.

The Aftermath

The fighting ended with both Kuwait and Iraq badly damaged. Before they withdrew, the Iraqis set fire to most of Kuwait's operating oil wells, systematically blew up or set fire to major buildings in Kuwait City and destroyed the electrical power-generating plants. They had already looted whatever they could carry away. During the air campaign the Iraqis lost up to 80 per cent of their refining capacity; much of their power-generating capacity was put out of action; most of their transportation infrastructure, including the railways, major bridges to the south of Baghdad, and main roads were severely damaged; and their telecommunications system was put out of action.

It will take a generation for Iraq to recover from the onslaught. And it is likely that as long as Saddam Hussein remains in power they will continue to suffer. Iraqi funds are frozen world-wide and sanctions on certain strategic goods remain, including, of course, on weapons systems. Certain Iraqi funds are likely to be unfrozen so that essential food and medicines can be purchased. The UN has also approved the sale of some Iraqi oil providing the proceeds are paid into a UN-administered fund which can siphon off 30 per cent of the income earned to be paid to Kuwait in war reparations. The remaining income must be spent on essential supplies for the Iraqi people.

Saddam Hussein remains sufficiently strong, however, to be able to keep his people under control. The plight of the Iraqi Kurds in the months after the war was seen by millions on TV screens across the world. The allied response was quick and effective. Operation Safe Haven was launched which once again, only weeks after they had left southern Iraq, saw coalition troops back on Iraqi soil. This time, US, British, French and Dutch troops secured a salient in Iraqi Kurdistan via a base in Turkey which enabled them to lure the Kurds out of the mountains, where they were dying in thousands, back to the safety of the plains. So called 'safe havens' were established and, after some initial hesitation, the Kurds were sufficiently reassured to return to their homeland. Although a deal has not been finalized, it does seem that Saddam Hussein is willing to grant these unfortunate people a

General Norman Schwarzkopf waves goodbye as he leaves Saudi Arabia for the last time on 20 March 1991.

A Sea King helicopter from 846 the Royal Navy Air Squadron flies over blazing oil fields on the outskirts of Kuwait City on 7 March 1991. Saddam Hussein carried out his threat to set fire to the Kuwaiti oilfields before his forces withdrew in late February 1991. This was the first known instance of ecological warfare.

BE

Corporal Dominic McDonald from Aberdeen talks to an elderly Kurdish woman in northern Iraq. She stayed in her village Darhuzan, after all her neighbours had left for the Turkey/Iraq border in spring 1991. The United States, Britain and France sent forces into northern Iraq to create a 'safe haven' for the return of the Kurds to their homeland. The operation was a success and these forces withdrew in July 1991.

Opposite: Operation Safe Haven, to provide comfort, shelter and medical aid for hundreds of thousands of displaced Kurds, was launched soon after the end of the Gulf War. Here a Kurdish refugee struggles to carry his sick wife from an RAF Chinook helicopter. The couple were rescued from a camp inside Iraq and flown to Turkey for medical treatment in mid-April 1991.

Overleaf: Two French soldiers clear the beaches of Kuwait City of mines following the end of hostilities in March 1991.

degree of autonomy. Meanwhile, he threatens to suppress the Shias in the south of Iraq who also rose in revolt against his regime in the wake of the Gulf War.

However, whilst Saddam Hussein as President of the Republic of Iraq retains sufficient military strength to deal with any future opposition to his regime, he is no longer a threat to Middle East peace. A UN team is dismantling his remaining nuclear and chemical capability; his army is not strong enough to mount offensive action outside the borders of Iraq; the Soviet Union is no longer prepared to give unqualified support to his regime; substantive efforts are being made to solve the Palestinian issue; the bulk of his people no longer hold him in the same regard; the economy and infrastructure of Iraq are in tatters; his every move is watched by the UN and the Western nations. Although he remains in power, he is a marked man.

Whilst the political ramifications of the Gulf War were complex, the overall lesson for the world is clear: the United States is now the world's only superpower. Economic muscle alone is not enough: Japan and Germany remain influential but the US has emerged supreme. The Soviet Union has massive problems though, due largely to Mikhail Gorbachev, they retained some influence through the Gulf War. The events of August 1991 make the Soviet Union an even more uncertain entity in the future. The war highlighted national differences in Europe. The UK supported the US and succeeding in reviving the special relationship; France showed its preference for independent action; Germany agonized about the legal and political niceties of contributing troops; Belgium managed to distinguish itself by refusing to sell much-needed artillery ammunition to the UK, one of the more distasteful decisions of the war. The myth of the Arab unity was truly shattered by the war. Not only did one Arab nation invade another, but other Arab nations then welcomed US and Western troops on to their soil. The UN perhaps came out of it best of all, its credibility and influence much enhanced.

The Gulf War was an extraordinary event in history. A coalition decided to put a wrong right, it transported hundreds of thousands of men and vast tonnages of equipment halfway around the world, adapted them for desert warfare, trained extensively, honed a professional fighting machine to perfection, and then fought and won a battle. It will be recorded as one of the greatest campaigns ever fought. The Iraqi people were the chief victims and they continue to suffer while Saddam Hussein sits in Baghdad, unrepentant but shackled. The final act of this drama is yet to be played out.

A young Kuwaiti child holds aloft the flag of Kuwait during the victory celebrations following the liberation of Kuwait City in the last days of February 1991.

Overleaf: Republican Guard troops sitting atop an armoured car display a magazine cover of President Saddam Hussein before the mosque of Imam al-Ali in Nadjaf in Iraq on 1 April 1991 after putting down the revolt of Sunni Muslims in the south of Iraq. The soldier on the right has his hand on a Sagger anti-tank missile.

Opposite: The mother of United States marine Lance Corporal J. Lumplins weeps as she is escorted from her son's grave by marine staff following her son's funeral service on 16 February 1991. As is customary, she holds the flag which draped her son's coffin.

The tragedy of war. Grieving relatives at RAF Brize Norton in March 1991 await the bodies of their loved ones. HRH The Duke of Kent stands on the extreme left.

Opposite: The coffin of Corporal David Denbury is carried from an RAF Hercules transport plane at RAF Brize Norton after being flown home from the Gulf on 8 March 1991. Allied losses were astonishingly small; 141 dead, 479 casualties and 57 missing in action.

Tornado pilot, Flight Lieutenant John Peters reunited with his wife Helen, his two-year-old son, Guy, and six-month-old daughter, Toni, on 7 March 1991. He had been taken prisoner by the Iraqis and forced to appear on Iraqi television having been shot down over Iraq in the early days of the air offensive.

The citizens of Kuwait and Arab soldiers of the coalition celebrate the liberation of Kuwait City in March 1991.

Overleaf: The scene as Desert Rats return from the Gulf to RAF Gutersloh in Germany in March 1991.

Sources

Strategic Survey 1990–1991 (published by Brassey's for the International Institute for Strategic Studies, London, 1991)

Survival, March 1991 (published by Brassey's for the International Institute for Strategic Studies, London, 1991)

Air Clues, Volume 45, The Royal Air Force magazine (MOD, 1991)

The Gulf War, Terry Manners (Grosvenor Press, Portsmouth, 1991)

Desert War, Mike Moore (Penguin Books, London, 1991)

Numerous radio and newspaper reports

Appendix 1

The Gulf Crisis: Coalition Forces Order of Battle

(Excluding forces of Gulf Co-operation Council[a])

GROUND FORCES

DEPLOYED FOR OPERATIONS DESERT SHIELD, DESERT STORM AND DESERT SABRE

United States	Tanks	Artillery	Attack Helicopters
HQ 3rd Army			
HQ XVIIIth Airborne Corps			
82nd Airborne Division	–	54	18
101st Air Assault Division	–	54	70
1st Cavalry Division (two brigades only)	216	56	18
24th Mechanized Infantry Division	270	72	26
3rd Armoured Cavalry Regiment	129	42	26
XVIII Corps Artillery (one Brigade)	–	72	–
HQ VII Corps			
1st Armoured Division	324	80	44
3rd Armoured Division	324	80	44
1st Infantry Division (from CONUS – Continental USA) (with one brigade 2nd Armoured Division under command	270	72	26
2nd Armoured Cavalry Regiment	129	42	26
VII Corps Artillery (three brigades)	–	240	–
11th Combat Aviation Brigade	–	–	36
III Corps Artillery (two brigades)	–	144	–

United States	Tanks	Artillery	Attack Helicopters
7th Air Defence Artillery Brigade	–	–	–
11th Air Defence Artillery Brigade	–	–	–
12th Combat Aviation Brigade	–	–	18
5th Special Forces Group	–	–	–
1st Marine Expeditionary Force			
1st Marine Division (reinforced to four regiments) with under command one brigade 2nd Armoured Division	248	144	–
2nd Marine Division (two regiments)	140	120	48
Afloat			
4th Marine Expeditionary Brigade	50		8
5th Marine Expeditionary Brigade	ε50		8
13th Marine Expeditionary Unit	ε20		4
United Kingdom			
1st Armoured Division			
7th Armoured Brigade	117	24	2
4th Armoured Brigade	60	24	–
Divisional Artillery	–	40	–
Divisional Aviation	–	–	18
Armoured Reconnaissance Regiment	–	–	–
Special Forces:			
Elements 22nd Regiment SAS			
Elements SBS Royal Marines			
France			
6th 'Daguet' Light Armoured Division (one tank, two armoured reconnaissance, two infantry, one artillery, one engineer, two aviation regiments)	40	18	70
Egypt			
3rd Mechanized Division	200	70	–
4th Armoured Division	250	40	–
Syria			
9th Armoured Division	300	54	–
Special Forces Regiment	–	–	–
Czechoslovakia			
Chemical Defence Unit	–	–	–

DEPLOYED FOR OPERATION DESERT SHIELD ONLY

Pakistan: (some 10,000 men)

Two brigades (one equipped from Saudi Arabian stock-pile)

Bangladesh: (some 5,000 men) one infantry brigade and engineers
Morocco: (some 2,000 men) including Special Forces Unit
Niger: (some 500 men) infantry battalion
Senegal: (some 500 men)

NON-COMBAT UNITS DEPLOYED IN SAUDI ARABIA
Australia: Medical Team (on board USS *Comfort*)
Hungary: Medical Team
New Zealand: Two Medical Teams
Poland: Medical Unit
Singapore: Medical Team (with UK medical services)
Sweden: Field Hospital

AIR FORCES

(excluding transport aircraft)

DEPLOYED FOR OPERATIONS DESERT SHIELD, DESERT STORM AND DESERT SABRE

United States

US Air Force		
Fighters	F-15C/D *Eagle*	120
Fighter Ground Attack	F-15E *Eagle*	48
	F-16 *Fighting Falcon*	249
Close Air Support	A-10 *Warthog*	144
Fighter-Bombers	F-111E	80
	F-117A	44
Bombers	B-52	32
Electronic Warfare	EF-III *Raven*	18
	F-4G *Wildweasel*	48
AWACS	E-3A *Sentry*	5
Reconnaissance	RC-135	16
	U-2R	6
	RF-4C	2
	E-8A (JSTARS)	2
Tankers	KC-135	256
	KC-10	46
Special Forces	AC/EC/MC/HC-130	
	MH-53J *Pavelow*	50+

US Navy
6 Air Wings embarked on USS *America, John F. Kennedy, Midway, Ranger, Saratoga* and *Theodore Roosevelt*

Fighters	F-14E *Tomcat*/FA-18A *Hornet*	144

Fighter Ground Attack	FA-18A *Hornet*/A-7E *Corsair*	144
	A-6E *Intruder*	60
Electronic Warfare	EA-6B *Prowler*	24
AEW	E-2C *Hawkeye*	24
Tanker	KA-6D	24
US Marine Corps		
3rdMarineAircraftWing(reinforced)		
Fighter Ground Attack	FA-18 *Hornet*	132
	AV-8B *Harrier*	100
	A-6E *Intruder*	20
FAC	OV-10 *Bronco*	18
Electronic Warfare	EA-6B *Prowler*	15
Tanker	KC-13	nk
United Kingdom		
Fighters	*Tornado* F-3	18
Fighter Ground Attack	*Tornado* GR-1	42
	Jaguar	12
	Buccaneer	6
AEW (MR)	*Nimrod*	3
Tankers	VC-10	8
	Victor	6
	Tristar K-1	2
France		
Fighters	*Mirage* 2000C	14
	Mirage F-1C	8
Fighter Ground Attack	*Jaguar* A	28
Reconnaissance	*Mirage* F-1CR	6
Italy		
Fighter Ground Attack	*Tornado* 1DS	8
Canada		
Fighters	CF-18	26
Tanker	CC-137	1

NAVAL FORCES

(Ships of the US and UK Navies and the French DD *Jean de Vienne* took part in support of Operations Desert Storm and Desert Sabre, the remainder were deployed to implement the UN sanctions regime and to conduct minesweeping operations (listed separately). Amphibious and underway support ships are not included.)

ABBREVIATIONS

BB Battleship
CG Guided Missile Cruiser
CGN Nuclear Powered Guided Missile Cruiser

CV Carrier
CVN Nuclear Powered Carrier
DDG Guided Missile Destroyer
FF Frigate
FFG Guided Missile Frigate
SSN Nuclear Powered Submarine

United States

Carrier Battle Groups: 6

USS *America* Battle Group: CV *America*; CGN *Virginia*; CG *Normandy*; DDG *William V. Pratt, Preble*; FFG *Halyburton*

USS *Kennedy* Battle Group: CV *Kennedy*; CGN *Mississippi*; CG *Thomas S. Gates, San Jacinto*; DD *Moosbrugger*; FFG *Samuel B. Roberts*

USS *Midway* Battle Group: CV *Midway*; CG *Bunker Hill, Mobile Bay*; DD *Fife, Oldendorf*; FFG *Curts, Rodney M. Davies*.

USS *Ranger* Battle Group: CV *Ranger*; CG *Princeton, Valley Forge*; DD *Paul F. Foster, Harry W. Hill, Francis Hammond*

USS *Roosevelt* Battle Group: CVN *Theodore Roosevelt*, CG *Leyte Gulf, Richard K. Turner*; DD *Caron*; FFG *Hawes*; FF *Vreeland*

USS *Saratoga* Battle Group: CV *Saratoga*, CG *Belknap* (Flagship 6th Fleet) *Biddle, Philippine Sea*; DDG *Sampson*; DD *Spruance*; FF *Thomas C. Hart, Elmer Montgomery*

Other Forces

Command Ships: *La Salle, Blue Ridge*
Battleships: (2): BB *Missouri, Wisconsin*
Cruisers: (4): CG *Antietam, England, Horne, Worden*
Destroyers: (4): DDG *Kidd, Macdonough*; DD *David R. Ray, Leftwich*
Frigates: (9): FFG *Rentz, Robert G. Bradley, Taylor, Vandergrift, Ford, Jarret, McInerney, Nicholas*; FF *Barbey*
Submarines: (6): SSN *Louisville* plus about 5 others
Hospital Ships: *Comfort, Mercy*

United Kingdom

Destroyers: DDG *Cardiff, Gloucester, Manchester, Exeter*
Frigates: FF *Brazen, London, Brilliant, Brave*
Helicopter support/hospital ship: *Argus*
Submarines: *Otus, Opossum*
(UK force was in process of relief as Operation Desert Storm began)

DEPLOYED TO ENFORCE UN SANCTIONS

Argentina

Destroyer: *Almirante Brown/La Argentina*[b]
Frigate: *Spiro/Rosales*

Australia

Destroyer: *Brisbane*
Frigate: *Sydney*

Belgium

Frigate: *Wandelaar/Wielingen*[b]

Canada
Destroyer: *Athabaskan*
Frigate: *Terra Nova*
Denmark
Frigate: *Olfert Fischer*
France
Destroyers: *Du Chayla, La Motte-Picquet*
Frigates: *Commandant Bory, Doudart de Lagree, Premiere Maître L'Her, Protet*
Greece
Frigate: *Elli*
Italy
Destroyer: *Audace*
Frigates: *Libeccio, Zeffiro*
Netherlands
Frigates: *Jacob Van Heemskerck, Philips Van Almonde*
Fast combat support ship: *Zuiderkruis*
Norway
Armed Coast Guard ship: *Andenes*
Poland
Hospital ship: *Wodnik*
Rescue ship: *Piast*
Spain
Frigate: *Numancia/Reina Sofia*
Corvettes: *Diana, Infanta Cristina*

MINESWEEPING FORCES
(deployed in the Gulf during Operations Desert Storm and Desert Sabre)
United States
MCO: *Avenger*, MSO: *Adroit, Impervious, Leader* plus squadron six MH-53 helicopters
United Kingdom
Ocean Survey Ship (HQ): *Herald/Hecla*[b]
MHC: *Atherstone, Cattistock, Dulverton, Hurworth, Ledbury, Brocklesby, Bicester, Brecon*

MINESWEEPING FORCES (deployed to Gulf post 28 Feb 91)
Belgium
MHC: *Iris, Dianthus, Myosotis*
Support ship: *Zinnia*
France
MCM: *L'Aigle, Pégase, Orion, Sagittaire*
Diving support ship: *Pluton*
Germany
MHC: *Koblenz, Göttingen, Marburg*
MSC: *Schleswig Paderborn* (with *troika* minesweeping drones)
Support ship: *Donau*

Italy

MHC: *Milazzo, Sapri, Vieste*
Support ship: *Tremiti*
3 MCM

Netherlands

MHC: *Haarlem, Harlingen, Zierikzee*

Australia

Support ship: *Westralia* with diving team on board

Japan

MCC: *4 Yurishima, Hikoshima, Awashima, Sakushima*
MCM support ship: *Hayase*

[a] For forces of Gulf Co-operation Council see listings in Country Section of *The Military Balance* (International Institute for Strategic Studies, London, 1991)
[b] Ship reliefs took place during period Jan to Feb

Appendix 2

The Gulf Crisis: Main Financial Contributions

(both to the cost of the war, and to compensate for economic loss caused by the war (in $billion)

Pledged by	Financial Aid To				In Kind
	US	UK	Turkey/Egypt	Other	Aid
Saudi Arabia	16.80	0.56	2.85	1.77	ε6.0[a]
Kuwait[b]	16.01	1.32	2.50	2.18[c]	–
UAE	3.50	0.50	0.85	0.62	0.14[a]
European Community	–	–	0.80	–	–
France	–	0.175	0.20	0.03	–
Germany	6.57	0.60	1.19	0.94[d]	0.53
Italy	0.45	–	0.65	–	–
Other EC	–	0.02	0.19	–	–
Japan	10.74	–	2.13	0.10	0.46
South Korea	0.37	–	0.10	0.02	0.02
Norway	–	–	0.02	0.08	–
Switzerland	–	–	0.12	–	–
Other	–	–	0.17	–	–

[a] Cost of supply for petrol, water and other services to Coalition forces
[b] Does not include debt forgiveness to Egypt worth est $4 billion
[c] Includes $1 billion aid to France
[d] Includes $800 million aid to Israel

Picture Credits

The Press Association: 4–5, 8–9, 11–15, 31–3, 37–42, 47, 56–9, 65, 68–9, 71–8.

AFP: 1–3, 6–7, 10, 24–30, 34–6, 43–5, 48–55, 60–2, 64, 66–7, 70.

Royal Navy. 16, 19–23, 63.

Index

References in *italic* indicate illustrations.